*Citrus Rice with Fresh
- lemon J/zest ½
- lime J/zest ½
- orange J/zest ½
- 2 tbs. Parsley
- 1½ cup Basmati Rice long grain
- 2¾ cup Water
  or Stock
- white Pepper ¼ tsp.
- K. Salt ½ tsp.

uctions

itrus Soy Glaze

Glaze
- Soy Sauce 2 tbs
- Sesame oil 2 tsp.
- Scalion 1 tbs.
- lemon Juice 1 lemon
- Water 1 tbs

Olive oil -
- Rosemary/
- Garlic -
- Salt - 1 lb
- Pepper - ¼ tsp
- Paprika - 1 tsp
- 4 lemon Wedges
- Large shrimp 1½ lb
- Rosemary 2 tbs

Oil 3 Rosemary
Paprika Roasted Shrimp
Rosemary/ 3 sprigs Grilled 3-27-11
5 cloves leaves off Directions
No Paper

*Roasted Red Potato Wedges w/ garlic
Thyme infused olive oil. *Instructions
Potatoes
- Red Potatoes - 2 lbs
- Salt - ½ tsp
- Pepper - ½ tsp

25
425°

Olive Oil
- Olive oil - ⅓ cup
- Garlic - 3 cloves
- thyme - 1 tbs

Instructions *Marinara
- Tomato - 3 lbs
- Olive oil - ¼ cup
- Garlic - 2 cloves
- Yellow onion - ½ medium onion
- Red Pepper Flake - ⅛ tsp
- Basil - ¼ cup
- Salt - ½ tsp
- Black Pepper - ¼ t
- Parsley - ¼ t
- Dried ore
- Sugar - 1 tsp
- Bay leaf - 1

cacia

*Instructions

*Cheesy Mashed Potato with
Bacon Crumbles *Instruct
- Yukon Gold
- Yellow Potato - 2 Lbs
- Milk - 1 cup
- Butter - 3 tbs
- Cheddar - 6 oz. 1 cup
- Parmesan - 3 oz.
- Black Pepper - ⅛ tsp.
- Salt - ¼ tsp
- Bacon - 6 slices
- Garlic - 4 cloves

- Cook Bacon
- Cook Potatoes
  in Water 15 Min
- Drain, Return low Heat
- Add Everything.

To Gale,

It was great meeting you. I hope you enjoy my book!

Best Regards,

Stick It in Your Pie Hole

A Book of California Cuisine

Jake Tanner

Dedications

To my Grandpa, Dr. David Baer, his love for food and gourmet cooking inspired me. He taught me so much and I will cherish our relationship forever. For the past three years we discussed the progress I was making on my cookbook, he unfortunately just past away several months before the release of my book. I love you Grandpa Baer. You are the driving force behind the passion I have put into this book.

To my family, the other four JT's, Jim, Janus, Jolene, and Jordan, thank you for the support and the motivation to keep me doing what I love.

To all of my extended family for their interest and support throughout the writing of this special book.

To all of my friends who supported my unique talent.

To Chef Samson Francois, who took me under his wing and gave me the opportunities necessary to develop my career. Without him I would have missed the formal training I needed to write this book.

I have been so fortunate to have the support of many people in my life, you are all great. I appreciate all of the encouragement I have received from the bottom of my heart.

Contents

Introduction

Cooking is like music. Not in the literal way where the potatoes play guitar then the broccoli joins in and sings. They are similar in the way that the artist expresses himself. Just as a musician can be bold and daring with his music, a good cook can be bold when preparing a sauce and daring when plating food. Cooking is exciting, it is invigorating and refreshing. Cooking is my medium for expression. I hear many contemporary musicians talk about how they want their music to tell their story—their album to form a connection with their listeners. As a 17 year old chef, that is exactly how I approach cooking.

The recipes in this book convey my passion for food and my story as a young food enthusiast. I allow the themes of my childhood to guide me on this culinary adventure, to give me the inspiration, desire, and knowledge to write a cookbook that reflects on my life and love for great food.

There are no boundaries in cooking. Cooking is cross-cultural and multi-generational. Cooking is such that no matter who writes the recipes, what age they are, or what national origin the food is, anyone can embrace it. This is the basis for California Cuisine. It is a menu that delivers both the liveliest of wholesome food and satisfying flavors, the freshest ingredients, and a menu that appeals across a wide range of palates. California Cuisine is food that simply tastes good and is good for you. It is a mix of countries and ingredients, people and ages, enjoyed in any home around the world.

I want the readers to know that this book is more than a collection of my recipes. When you try these great dishes you will discover the enthusiasm that is in each and every dish. You will know my story and you will know the joys of cooking and sharing food with friends and family. There is love, fusion, tradition, artistry, fresh and new flavors, and what I consider the most important, my passion for creating, sharing, and eating food.

Before You Begin...

1. I have written, tested, and photographed each of the recipes in this book, they are 100% original.

2. Be prepared to experience my obsessions with the robust flavors of citrus, garlic, herbs, and spices.

3. All of the recipes in this book are written to feed four people. (Plus or minus one or two depending on how hungry your diners are.)

4. *"Mise en place"* ... What in the world does this fun French term mean? It directly translates to "everything in its place." This means that before you start any cooking, you will need to measure and prepare the ingredients that will be used in the recipe. Preparing *mise en place* is the first step for EVERY recipe in this book. This most important step gives you the power to complete the dish much faster *and I guarantee that your food will taste better!*

RADISH
$1.50/bun

BEETS
$1.50/bunch

Salad & Dressing

Cobb Salad "Tower"

Most cobb salads are prepared with bleu cheese dressing; in this one I have tried a healthy twist with the balsamic vinaigrette. Where did the inspiration come from? Well just the fact that I am not the biggest bleu cheese fan did the trick. But if you will miss it, feel free to sprinkle some bleu cheese on top.

Ingredient	Amount
Salad	-
Iceberg Lettuce	1 Head- Finely Shredded
Tomato	1 Cup- Diced
Green Onion/ Scallion	2 Tablespoons- Finely Sliced
Avocado	1-Thinly Sliced
Hard Boiled Eggs	2- Finely Chopped
Bacon	4 Slices- Crisped & Broken to Bits
Cooked Chicken Meat	2 Cups- Shredded
Dressing	-
Reduced Balsamic Vinaigrette	1 Recipe on Page 25

Directions

-Prepare *mise en place*.
-Prepare the Reduced Balsamic Vinaigrette according to the directions on page 25.
-Take a large, empty soup can and using a can opener that leaves no sharp edges, remove the top and bottom from the can. You can also try using a large paper cup with the bottom removed. (Leaving only a hollow cylinder)
-Place the hollow cylinder on a plate and individually layer each ingredient inside the cylinder. If you are using a paper cup place the wide part down. I like the following order, lettuce, tomato, chicken, and hard boiled eggs.
-After the ingredients are in the cylinder, gently pack down the ingredients, and then slowly pull the cylinder up and away from the tower of ingredients.
-Garnish with the bacon, avocado, and scallion.
- Drizzle the dressing over the salad.
-Enjoy!

Summer Vegetable Salad

Simple, easy, clean, fresh and colorful...this dish is just great. My grandma makes a salad that is very similar to this one; I tried to replicate her dressing exactly and though that really will never be possible, this salad is still incredibly tasty.

Ingredient	Amount
Salad	-
Cucumber	2 Cups- Cut to Small Cubes
Cherry Tomato	3 Cups- Cut to Halves
Yellow Bell Pepper	1 Large- Cut to Small Cubes
Kosher Salt	¼ Teaspoon
Dressing	-
Shallot Vinaigrette	1 Recipe on Page 27

Directions

-Prepare *mise en place.*
-Prepare the Shallot Vinaigrette according to the directions on page 27.
-In a large mixing bowl combine the cucumber, cherry tomatoes, yellow bell peppers, and kosher salt.
-Just before serving, toss the salad mixture with the dressing, or you may choose to prepare and plate the ingredients separately with the dressing poured on top. (As pictured)
-Enjoy!

"Working at the country club at age 11"

Field Greens and Pear Salad

When I was a young chef's apprentice at the local country club at age 11, the head chef, Samson Francois, taught me a wonderful pairing of pears, crunchy candied pecans, and grapes lavished on top of fresh mixed greens. This is an easy salad to master but it is so delicious and beautiful that it can be served at the fanciest of dinners or when you just want a great salad.

Ingredient	Amount
Salad	-
Mixed Field Greens	8 Packed Cups- Washed & Dried
Pear	1 Pear- Cut to Thin Slices
Candied Pecans or Walnuts	1/3 Cup
Grapes	½ Cup- Halved
Tomato	1 Large Tomato- Cut to 8 Slices
Dressing	-
White Wine Vinaigrette Or Lemon Rosemary Vinaigrette	1 Recipe on Page 29 1 Recipe on Page 31

Directions

-Prepare *mise en place*.
-Prepare the White Wine Vinaigrette according to the directions on page 29, or the Lemon Rosemary Vinaigrette according to the directions on page 31.
-In a large mixing bowl combine the mixed field greens, candied pecans, grapes, tomato and pear slices. (Save a few pear slices to garnish salads while plating.)
-Just before serving toss the salad mixture with your chosen dressing.
-Enjoy!

Roasted Beet Salad

If you have read this title and associated it with those canned beets, clear your mind and start again with fresh, slow roasted beets. The truth is that fresh, slowly roasted beets have a uniquely sweet flavor that is entirely unparalleled to canned beets. I am a big fan of lemon on fresh beets, so I have paired this dish with a fresh lemon rosemary vinaigrette.

Ingredient	Amount
Roasted Beets	-
Baby Beets	1 Pound- Stems Cut Off
Water	2 Cups
Red Onion	½ Medium Onion- Thinly sliced
Garlic	3 Cloves- Smashed
Dried Rosemary	2 Teaspoons
Brown Sugar	1/3 Cup
Kosher Salt	1 Teaspoon
Black Pepper	1 Teaspoon- Ground
Dressing	-
Lemon Rosemary Vinaigrette	1 Recipe on Page 31

Directions

-Prepare *mise en place.*
-Preheat your oven to 325 degrees.
-In a medium casserole dish mix the water, red onion, garlic, dried rosemary, brown sugar, kosher salt, and black pepper.
-Nestle the baby beets into the liquid, cover with aluminum foil, and place in the oven for 3 hours. Flip the beets halfway through cooking.
-During the last 20 minutes of cooking, you should prepare the Lemon Rosemary Vinaigrette on page 31.
-Remove the beets from the oven, and place them into a bath of ice water for 5 minutes.
-Remove the beets from the ice water, peel the outer skin off using your fingers, and quarter them.
-Plate, and drizzle with dressing.
-Enjoy!

Helpful Hints

-Plate on a small bed of lettuce if you are in the mood for some greens.

Caprese Salad Stack

Caprese salad is one of my favorite recipes in this book. It takes a few extra minutes to make your own dressings but the end product is a clean, fresh, and flavorful salad; one that resembles a fine restaurant in taste and a picture perfect presentation.

Ingredient	Amount
Caprese Salad	-
Beef Steak Tomato	4 Large- Cut Each Into 4 Even Slices
Fresh Mozzarella	8 Ounces- Cut Into 12 Slices
Fresh Basil	12 Whole Leaves
Kosher Salt	¼ Teaspoon
Black Pepper	½ Teaspoon- Ground
Dressings	-
Reduced Balsamic Vinaigrette	1 Recipe on Page 25
Modern Basil Pesto	1 Recipe on Page 127

Directions

-Prepare *mise en place.*
-Prepare the Modern Basil Pesto according to the instructions on page 127.
-Prepare the Reduced Balsamic Vinaigrette according to the instructions on page 25.
-Assemble the Caprese Stack by placing a slice of mozzarella, basil leaf, kosher salt, and black pepper between each layer of tomato. (There should be 3 layers, in between 4 slices of tomato)
-Insert one toothpick into each "corner" of the caprese sandwich, cut into quarters.
-Drizzle the top with Reduced Balsamic Vinaigrette and Modern Basil Pesto.
-Enjoy!

Chinese Chopped Salad

The great thing about this Chinese Chopped Salad is how it thrives on its simplicity. The nice part is that you have the choice of making the ingredients fresh, or if you are in a hurry you can always purchase premade fried wonton pieces and the crispy rice noodles. The ingredients have such a nice flavor and texture, all that's needed for the dressing is just a little bit of soy sauce and sesame oil.

Ingredient	Amount
Salad	-
Iceberg Lettuce	1 Head-Thinly Shredded
Fresh Cilantro	2 Tablespoons-Thinly Sliced
Roasted Almonds	¼ Cup- Finely Chopped
Roasted Sesame Seeds	¼ Cup
Fried Wonton Pieces	⅓ Cup
Crispy Rice Noodles	½ Cup- Broken to Small Pieces
Dressing	-
Soy Sauce	1 Tablespoon + 1 Teaspoon
Sesame Oil	1 Teaspoon

Directions

-Prepare *mise en place.*
-In a large mixing bowl combine the lettuce, cilantro, roasted almonds, and sesame seeds.
-Just before serving, mix the ingredients with the dressing.
-After the salad has been plated, sprinkle the fried wonton pieces and crispy rice noodles on top.
-Enjoy!

Helpful Hints

-If you cannot find crispy wonton pieces, you can make them yourself by thinly slicing eggroll skins, and frying them in 350 degree oil until they are golden brown and crunchy (about 1-2 minutes).
-The same goes for the crispy rice noodles (sometimes called Pad Thai noodles). These will fry quickly in about 10 seconds.
-Adding the dressing at the end preserves the crispness of the lettuce, and adding the fried noodles and wonton skins on top will help them to keep their crunch.

Reduced Balsamic Vinaigrette

This is a bold version of the ever faithful standard salad dressing. The trick to making this accompaniment is to whisk quickly while pouring in the olive oil extra slowly.

Ingredient	Amount
Reduced Balsamic	-
Balsamic Vinegar	⅓ Cup
Vinaigrette	-
Olive Oil	⅓ Cup
Kosher Salt	¼ Teaspoon
Black Pepper	¼ Teaspoon- Ground

Directions

-Prepare *mise en place.*
-Pour the balsamic vinegar into a small saucepan, and place over medium heat.
-Let cook for 10-15 minutes or until the mixture is half of its original volume.
-Pour the reduced balsamic into a medium bowl.
-Add the kosher salt, and black pepper to the reduced balsamic.
-Vigorously whisk the vinegar mixture while slowing pouring in the olive oil. Whisk until the mixture has completely come together and slightly thickened.
-Enjoy!

Shallot Vinaigrette

This dressing is extremely light and refreshing. I sure do think that I have come close to replicating grandma's famous version. Mix this dressing into any tossed vegetables for a quick, delicious, and fresh salad.

Ingredient	Amount
Vinaigrette	-
Shallot	1 Medium Size- Thinly Sliced
Garlic	2 Cloves- Thinly Sliced
Lemon	Juice of 2 Lemons
Olive Oil	⅓ Cup
Kosher Salt	¼ Teaspoon
Black Pepper	¼ Teaspoon- Ground

Directions

-Prepare *mise en place.*
-Combine the shallot, garlic, lemon juice, olive oil, kosher salt, and black pepper in a bowl.
-Gently mix.
-Let the mixture sit for 20 minutes, gently mix.
-Strain the liquid away from the solids.
-Mix the remaining liquid vigorously to emulsify the dressing.
-Enjoy!

White Wine Vinaigrette

This deliciously sweet vinaigrette goes perfectly with my field greens and pear salad. If you're looking to put new life into your lunchtime salad, give this recipe a shot.

Ingredient	Amount
Vinaigrette	-
White Wine Vinegar	3 Tablespoons
Olive Oil	⅓ Cup
Honey	½ Teaspoon
Kosher Salt	¼ Teaspoon
White Pepper	¼ Teaspoon- Ground

Directions

-Prepare *mise en place.*
-Combine the white wine vinegar, honey, kosher salt, and white pepper in a medium bowl.
-Vigorously mix as you slowly pour in the olive oil to emulsify the dressing.
-Enjoy!

Lemon Rosemary Vinaigrette

I love this lemon and rosemary combination. It is a simple mix of great flavors and I am sure it will be a new regular dressing in your house.

Ingredient	Amount
Vinaigrette	-
Lemon	Juice & Zest of 2
Fresh or Dried Rosemary	1 Tablespoon- Roughly Chopped
Olive Oil	⅓ Cup
Garlic	2 Cloves- Thinly Sliced
Kosher Salt	¼ Teaspoon
Black Pepper	¼ Teaspoon- Ground

Directions

-Prepare *mise en place.*
-Combine the lemon juice and zest, rosemary, olive oil, garlic, kosher salt, and black pepper in a bowl.
-Gently mix.
-Let the mixture sit for 20 minutes. Gently mix.
-Strain the liquid away from the solids.
-Mix the remaining liquid vigorously to emulsify the dressing.
-Enjoy!

Whole Grain Mustard Vinaigrette

I enjoy cooking with whole grain mustard because of the depth of flavor that it provides to any dish. Try pouring this dressing over simply grilled salmon or chicken.

Ingredient	Amount
Vinaigrette	-
Whole Grain Mustard	2 Teaspoons
Olive Oil	⅓ Cup
Balsamic Vinegar	1 Teaspoon
Fresh Cilantro	2 Teaspoons- Finely Minced
Fresh Parsley	2 Teaspoons- Finely Minced
Kosher Salt	¼ Teaspoon
Black Pepper	¼ Teaspoon- Ground

Directions

-Prepare *mise en place.*
-Combine the whole grain mustard, balsamic vinegar, cilantro, parsley, kosher salt, and black pepper in a bowl.
-Vigorously mix while you pour in the olive oil to emulsify the dressing.
-Enjoy!

Beef

Charbroiled Rib Eye

Wait. Don't even think about flipping this page until you consider making this charbroiled rib eye. There are three special words that describe this dish and that's all you will need to be hooked... juicy, succulent, and the third? Well, you will just have to decide that one for yourself...

Ingredient	Amount
Marinade	-
Olive Oil	1 Tablespoon
Vegetable or Canola Oil	1 Tablespoon
Red Onion	¼ Onion- Cut to Wedges
Garlic	2 Cloves- Smashed
Kosher Salt	½ Teaspoon
Black Pepper	¼ Teaspoon- Ground
Rib Eye Steaks	2 Large Rib Eye (About 1 Lb. each)
Worcestershire Sauce	2 Tablespoons

Directions

-Prepare *mise en place.*
-In a large plastic zip top bag combine the olive oil, vegetable or canola oil, red onion, and garlic.
-Sprinkle both sides of the rib eye with kosher salt and black pepper. Put the rib eyes into the bag of marinade.
-Let marinate for 30 minutes, being sure to flip the bag half way through the marinating time.
-While the rib eyes are marinating, preheat your charcoal grill to high. (If you do not have a charcoal grill, a gas grill, or an indoor grill pan will work.)
-Place the rib eyes on the grill, and cook for 2 minutes, rotate 45 degrees, and cook for another 2 minutes.
-Flip the rib eyes and cook for about 2 more minutes. (Cooking time will total about 6 minutes for medium doneness.)
-Remove the rib eyes from the grill and let sit for 5 minutes to rest.
-Pour the Worcestershire sauce over the rib eye. You may also serve the Worcestershire sauce on the side.
-Enjoy!

New York Burgers with Parmesan Frico

For some mind boggling reason, the typical burger in America has become a thin, hard, bland, and occasionally gross piece of meat, (sometimes resembling a piece of cardboard tossed between two buns). This burger recipe will change your mind about your favorite burger joint. These New York burgers combine bold flavor with complementary textures. Hold on tight and prepare to be mind blown.

Ingredient	Amount
Burger	-
Breadcrumbs	⅓ Cup
Parmesan Cheese	⅓ Cup- Shredded
Parsley	2 Tablespoons- Chopped
Eggs	2
Worcestershire Sauce	1 Tablespoon
Olive Oil	2 Tablespoons
Kosher Salt	½ Teaspoon
Black Pepper	1 Teaspoon- Ground
New York Steaks	1 ½ Pounds- Ground
Sesame Burger Buns	4
Parmesan Frico	-
Parmesan Cheese	8 Tablespoons- Shredded
Black Pepper	1 Teaspoon- Coarsely Ground

Directions

-Prepare *mise en place*.
-Combine the breadcrumbs, ⅓ cup parmesan, parsley, eggs, Worcestershire, olive oil, kosher salt, black pepper, and ground New York steaks in a large bowl.
-Use your hands to thoroughly mix all of the ingredients.
-Preheat your grill to medium high heat. (you may also use an indoor grill pan)
-Shape the meat in the bowl into a ball and then divide into 4 even portions.
-Pick up one portion, use your palms to roll it into a ball, and then place it onto wax paper. Begin to gently flatten the ball into a burger patty shape about ¾ inch thick. Use your thumb to gently push the center of the patty downwards to make a slight concave shape in the center. This will help keep the burger flat during cooking. (Without making the concave shape, the burger may form a bubble shape in the center.)
-Repeat this with the remaining 3 portions of meat.
-Place 2 tablespoons of paremesan for each frico onto a nonstick baking sheet, use your fingers to spread into an even disk. Sprinkle the top with pepper, and bake in a 375 degree oven for 7-10 minutes or until golden brown.
-Place the burgers on the grill and cook for 3-4 minutes.
-Flip and cook for another 2-3 minutes. The exact cooking time will depend on how thick you made your burgers and how you personally like them to be cooked.
-Enjoy!

Helpful Hints

-You can ask your butcher to grind the New York steaks for you.
-I always like to wear plastic disposable gloves when putting my hands in contact with raw meat.

Grilled Beef Skewers

This dish is great for entertaining company; it can be prepared ahead of time and is the ultimate finger food. The inspiration for these grilled beef skewers was a great dinner I had one night at a Korean barbeque restaurant. These skewers are my interpretation of that meal. If you are looking for a flavorful, pleasantly salty, and unique dish, search no more.

Ingredient	Amount
Marinade	-
Garlic	3 Cloves- Minced
Fresh Ginger	2 Inch Piece- Thinly Sliced
Fresh Cilantro	2 Tablespoons- Minced
Fresh Scallions	2 Tablespoons- Thinly Sliced
Soy Sauce	¼ Cup
Teriyaki Sauce	¼ Cup
Peanut or Vegetable Oil	2 Tablespoons
Black Pepper	½ Teaspoon- Ground
Flank Steak	1 ½ Pounds

Directions

-Prepare *mise en place*.
-In a 1 gallon plastic zip top bag combine the garlic, ginger, cilantro, scallions, soy sauce, teriyaki sauce, oil, and black pepper.
-Lay the flank steak on a cutting board.
-Flank steak has long muscle fibers that all run the same way. You will want to cut perpendicular to these fibers. (known as cutting across the grain) This will shorten the connective tissue of the beef, making it more tender. Cut the flank steak into ¼ inch thick strips. (I prefer using a long knife like a chef's knife or boning knife.)
-Place the strips of meat into the bag of marinade.
-Seal the bag and rotate it to evenly distribute the marinade among the strips of flank steak, and then set the bag into a bowl.
-Marinate in the refrigerator for 1 hour. Be sure to flip the bag over halfway through the marinating time.
-After the hour, remove the meat from the refrigerator.
-Preheat your grill to high. You may also cook the meat inside on a grill pan. If you cook the meat inside, you may need to cook in batches so you do not overcrowd the pan.
-Using long wood skewers, prepare the beef by taking a wood skewer and one strip of meat. Insert the stick ½ inch from the edge of the piece of the meat. Weave the meat onto the skewer, poking it back and forth through the meat every ½- 1 inch until you reach the end of the strip of meat.
-Use your hands to make sure the woven strip of meat is evenly spread out on the length of the skewer.
-Evenly place the skewered meat on an oiled and cleaned grill grate. Be sure to place the skewers running diagonally to the way that the grill grates run. This will ensure that the meat is touching the grates in as many places as possible to create even charring.
-Depending on your desired doneness, cook the meat for 1-2 minutes per side.
-Serve immediately.
-Enjoy!

Helpful Hints

-When using wood skewers, soak the skewers in water 30 minutes before skewering the meat. This will help prevent the wood from incinerating on the grill. You can also place the handles of the skewers over aluminum foil to prevent the burning of the handles.
-For an easy dipping sauce combine 5 parts of teriyaki, 1 part soy sauce, 1 part finely mined cilantro, and 1 part thinly sliced scallion.

Chicken

Brined Chicken Breast with Modern Basil Pesto

Are you tired of plain grilled chicken? Try this great combination of common ingredients that will light up your poultry. I will warn you ahead of time, the chicken can get slightly spicy with the red pepper flakes. The spice of the chicken is cut very nicely by the refreshing pesto.

Ingredient	Amount
Brine	-
Water	1 Cup
Orange Juice	1 Cup
Lemon Juice	1 Tablespoon
Cilantro	1 Cup- Chopped
Granulated Sugar	1 Tablespoon
Red Pepper Flakes	½ Teaspoon
Kosher Salt	2 Teaspoons
Black Pepper	½ Teaspoon- Ground
Chicken Breast	4 Boneless Chicken Breasts
Modern Basil Pesto	-
Modern Basil Pesto	1 Recipe on Page 127

Directions

-Prepare *mise en place.*
-In a medium sauce pot combine the water, orange juice, granulated sugar, red pepper flakes, kosher salt, and black pepper.
-Bring the brine to a boil over a medium high heat. Once it boils, turn the heat off, and mix thoroughly. Let the mixture sit for 20 minutes to cool down.
-Add the lemon juice and cilantro to the cooled brine.
-Pour the brine into a large plastic zip top bag and place the chicken breasts into the brine. Place in the refrigerator and let sit for 2 hours. Flip the bag every 30 minutes.
-Remove the chicken from the refrigerator.
-Preheat your grill to medium heat.
-Prepare the Modern Basil Pesto according to the directions on page 127.
-Place the chicken on the cleaned and oiled grill grate, and let cook for 3 minutes. Rotate 45 degrees, (to make a diamond grill pattern on the chicken) and let cook for another 3 minutes.
-Flip the chicken, and cook for 2 more minutes, rotate 45 degrees and cook for another 2 minutes or until the internal temperature has reached 160 degrees.
-Serve with the Modern Basil Pesto.
-Enjoy!

Helpful Hints

-This dish pairs very nicely with roasted potatoes. You can serve extra pesto on the side of the roasted potatoes.
-If you do not have an outdoor grill, this can be cooked inside on a grill pan, though I do recommend the outdoor grill.

Chicken Dumplings with Citrus Soy Glaze

Though the title may sound complex, I have found a way to make fresh dumplings with only about 30 minutes of prep time. The trick? Premade dumpling skins. This underutilized ingredient is just simply great. They are inexpensive, tasty, and easy to use. Want to impress your friends? Serve them a dish of chicken dumplings with citrus soy glaze, or better yet, get the group together for the prep and call it a culinary party.

Ingredient	Amount
Dumpling Filling	-
Cilantro	1 Tablespoon- Finely Chopped
Scallions (Green Onion)	1 Tablespoon- Finely Sliced
Soy Sauce	1 Tablespoon
Sesame Oil	2 Teaspoons
Ground Chicken	1 Pound Package
Premade Dumpling Skins	48
Black Pepper	¼ Teaspoon- Ground
Citrus Soy Glaze	-
Soy Sauce	3 Tablespoons
Sesame Oil	2 Teaspoons
Scallion	1 Tablespoon- Thinly Sliced
Lemon	Juice of 1
Water	1 Tablespoon

Directions

-Prepare *mise en place.*
-In a large bowl combine the filling: ground chicken, cilantro, scallions, soy sauce, sesame oil, and black pepper.
-Mix until all of the ingredients are thoroughly integrated with each other.
-In a separate bowl mix the dipping sauce by combining the soy sauce, sesame oil, scallion, lemon juice, and water. Set aside.
-Place the dumpling skins on one corner of the cutting board, and cover them with a moist (not wet) paper or tea towel. (If you use egg roll skins, be sure to cut them into quarters.)
-Place a small bowl of water on the cutting board.
-Place 4-5 dumpling skins in a row along the bottom of your board.
-Using a 1 teaspoon scoop, place 1 teaspoon of filling onto the center of each skin.
-Dip your finger into the water, and lightly wet all four outer edges of each dumpling skin.
-Using both hands, grab opposite corners on the skin, pull them together, and pinch at the top.
-Repeat on the remaining two corners; pinching the remaining two corners at the top with the first two.
-Pinch along the 4 seams of the dumpling to ensure that you have completely sealed it.
-Repeat those steps until all of the dumplings have been formed.
-Place a large fry pan over medium high heat.
-Pour 1 Tablespoon of vegetable or peanut oil in the pan.
-Place the dumplings onto the pan (you will need to cook them in 2-3 batches).
-Let them cook until the bottoms are browned, about 3-4 minutes.
-Once the bottoms are browned, place about 3-4 large ice cubes into the center of the pan, and immediately cover with a large bowl, or lid. (one that will cover over all of the dumplings) The ice cubes are going to slowly melt on the pan and the bowl or lid will create your own instant steamer.
-Let the dumplings steam for about 3 minutes, or until the internal temperature has reached 165 degrees.
-Whisk the dipping sauce, and serve alongside the dumplings.

-Enjoy!

Lemon Chicken Breast with Heirloom Tomato & Baby Spinach Salad

I am one of those people who hate the consistency of boiled chicken, but love the texture of grilled. With this lemon chicken, I have you flatten the chicken breast so that you can grill it quickly over high heat to develop that great char on it. This gives it that special added flavor and a little crunch. By placing the freshly grilled chicken on the spinach salad, you are able to slightly wilt the spinach giving you a unique mix of textures. This recipe has it all, simplicity, great texture, fresh ingredients, and bold flavor.
Absolutely one of my favorites in this book.

Ingredient	Amount
Marinade	-
Fresh or Dried Rosemary	1 Tablespoon- Chopped
Garlic	3 Cloves- Minced
Lemon	Juice & Zest of 1
Lime	Juice & Zest of 2
Olive Oil	3 Tablespoons
Kosher Salt	¼ Teaspoon
Black Pepper	½ Teaspoon
Boneless Chicken Breast	4 Breasts- Cleaned & Flattened
Parmesan Cheese	⅓ Cup- Shredded
Baby Spinach Salad	-
Baby Spinach	1 Handful Per Plate
Heirloom Tomato	1 Cup- Diced
Vinaigrette	-
Olive Oil	⅓ Cup
Lemon	Juice of 1
Balsamic Vinegar	2 Tablespoons

Directions

-Prepare *mise en place.*
-In a large plastic zip top bag combine the rosemary, garlic, lemon juice and zest, lime juice and zest, olive oil, kosher salt, and black pepper.
-Place the flattened chicken breasts in the bag of marinade, seal the bag, and rotate it so the marinade becomes evenly distributed around the chicken.
-Place the bag of marinating chicken into a bowl and move it to the refrigerator.
-Let the chicken marinate for 1-2 hours, flipping the bag every 30 minutes.
-Remove the chicken from the refrigerator, and preheat your grill to high. You may also choose to cook the chicken inside using a grill pan.
-Prepare a plate for each diner with a handful of baby spinach and the diced heirloom tomatoes.
-To prepare the vinaigrette, pour the lemon juice and balsamic vinegar into a medium bowl.

-Vigorously whisk the vinegar mixture while slowly pouring in the olive oil. Whisk until the mixture has completely emulsified.
-To cook the chicken, place it on the grill. Let it sit for 1 minute, rotate the chicken 45 degrees, and cook for another minute. (this will create diamond shaped grill marks)
-Flip the chicken, cook for 1 minute, rotate 45 degrees like before, and cook for 1 more minute or until cooked throughout.
-During the last minute of grilling, sprinkle each breast with the parmesan cheese, and remove from the grill.
-Pour the vinaigrette on the salad (about 1-2 tablespoons for each salad) and plate the chicken breast on top of the salad.
-Serve immediately.
-Enjoy!

Helpful Hints

-By placing the bag of marinating chicken into a bowl, it will help prevent spills.
-An easy way to oil the grill grates is to take an onion, cut it in half, grip it between long tongs, generously pour oil onto the cut side of the onion, and rub the hot grill with the onion. This will do three things:
*Oils the grates evenly.
*Cleans burnt scum off the grill.
*Leaves a nice flavor on the grill.
-For a peppery bite, try using arugula in the salad instead of the baby spinach.

Chicken Picatta

I am a die hard chicken picatta fan. For those of you who have never had it before, it is thin chicken cutlets sautéed in olive oil and butter, and then simmered in a lemon, garlic, and caper sauce. It is simple, clean, fresh, and just delicious. I love this dish so much; I knew I had to include my own rendition of it in my book. Enjoy!

Ingredient	Amount
Chicken	-
Butter	3 Tablespoons- Softened
Olive Oil	2 Tablespoons
Kosher Salt	¼ Teaspoon
Black Pepper	¼ Teaspoon- Ground
Chicken Breast	2 Medium Chicken Breasts- Butterflied, and pounded to ¼ inch thickness.
All Purpose flour	½ Cup
Sauce	-
Lemon	Juice of 2 lemons
Chicken Stock	½ Cup
Capers	2 Tablespoons- Rinsed & Drained
Garlic	3 Cloves- Finely Minced
Butter	2 Tablespoons
Garnish	-
Parsley	1 Tablespoon
Lemon	Zest of 1

Directions

-Prepare *mise en place*.
-Sprinkle the butterflied and flattened chicken breast with kosher salt and black pepper.
-Place the flour on a plate, and then dredge each piece of chicken in the flour, evenly coating on both sides. Set the prepared chicken aside.
-Preheat a large skillet to medium-high heat.
-Place 3 tablespoons of butter and the olive oil in the pan. Distribute the fat evenly throughout the pan.
-Place the dredged chicken breast in the pan. Make sure not to over crowd the pan, if you need to cook the chicken in two batches that is fine.
-Cook the chicken for 3 minutes, flip, and cook for another 3 minutes.
-Remove the chicken from the pan, and set aside on a plate.
-Turn the heat to high. (There will be extra fat in the bottom of the pan, this will add to the sauce)
-Pour in the lemon juice, chicken stock, capers, and garlic. Bring to a boil for 1 minute, whisking occasionally.
-Reduce heat to low, and put the chicken back into the pan.
-Simmer the chicken in the sauce for 5 minutes, making sure to flip the chicken half way through the simmering process.
-Turn off the heat and plate the chicken
-Melt the remaining 2 tablespoons of butter into the sauce. Whisk to melt evenly.
-Pour the sauce over the plated chicken.
-Garnish with parsley and lemon zest.
-Enjoy!

Tuscan Flared Roasted Chicken

This luscious chicken is smothered in fresh herbs and roasted to perfection, chicken at its best.

Ingredient	Amount
Herb Paste	-
Fresh Rosemary	1 Tablespoon- Finely Minced
Fresh Thyme	10 Sprigs
Coriander	1 Teaspoon- Ground
Garlic	10 Cloves (3 Minced, 7 Halved)
Paprika	1 Teaspoon
Olive Oil	5 Tablespoons- Divided
Kosher Salt	1 Teaspoon
Black Pepper	1 Teaspoon- Ground
Chicken	1 Whole Chicken
Lemon	1 Lemon- Cut to 4 Wedges

Directions

-Prepare *mise en place*.

-Place the whole chicken on a cutting board, using either kitchen shears or a boning knife; remove the backbone of the chicken. (You can ask your butcher to do this for you.)

-Place the chicken skin-side up on the cutting board. Using your hands, push down on the sternum of the chicken to make it lay completely flat.

-In a medium bowl combine the rosemary, coriander, 3 minced cloves of garlic, paprika, and 2 tablespoons of olive oil. Mix to combine.

-Evenly sprinkle both sides of the chicken with kosher salt and black pepper.

-Rub the herb paste on both sides of the chicken.

- Preheat your oven to 400 degrees.

-Preheat a large pan on medium-high heat and add the remaining 3 tablespoons of olive oil into the pan.

-Add the remaining 7 cloves of garlic and the whole sprigs of thyme to the pan, cook for 1 minute to infuse the flavor into the olive oil.

-Push the garlic and thyme to the outer edges of the pan.

-Place the chicken, skin-side down into the pan, and place a weight on it. (To do this, I place a sheet of foil on top of the chicken, and then place a pot half filled with water on top of the foil.) The weight will help create a nice crust on the chicken.

-Let the chicken cook for 7-12 minutes or until it is golden brown.

-Flip the chicken, place the weight on as before. Cook the underside for another 7-10 minutes.

-Remove the chicken from the pan and place it on a roasting pan. Place in the oven for 20-40 minutes or until the internal temperature has reached 160 degrees.

-Remove the chicken from the oven, cover with foil, and let rest for 10 minutes before serving.

-Serve the roasted chicken with lemon wedges.

-Enjoy!

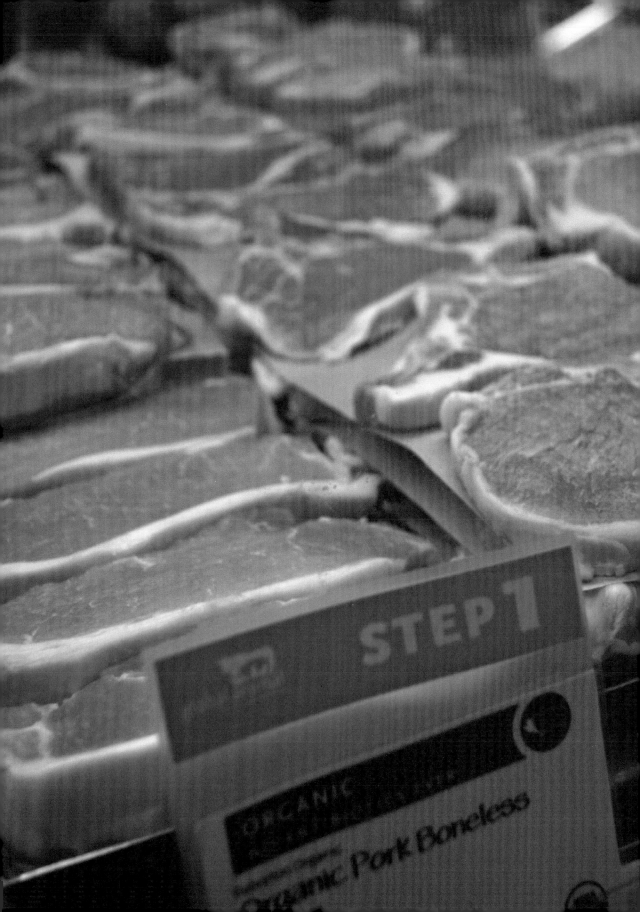

Pork

Mustard Glazed Pork Chop with Jicama Salad

The seed of the mustard plant is a spice that hides in a condiment jar in most Americans' refrigerator waiting to be plastered onto yet another hotdog. It's time to liberate that great seed and put it to good use. You must try it in this perfectly seasoned pork chop.

Ingredient	Amount
Marinade	-
Thyme	1 Teaspoon- Ground
Whole Grain Mustard	1 Tablespoon
Garlic	3 Cloves- Minced
Lime	Juice of 3 Large Limes
Olive Oil	3 Tablespoons
Kosher Salt	1 Teaspoon
Black Pepper	½ Teaspoon- Ground
Pork Tenderloin	1 ½ Pound Loin- Cut to 4 Even Chops
Jicama Salad	-
Jicama	½ of a Large Jicama- Diced
Cilantro	3 Tablespoons- Finely Minced
Lime	Juice & Zest of 1

Directions

-Prepare *mise en place.*
-Combine the thyme, whole grain mustard, garlic, lime, olive oil, kosher salt, and black pepper in a bowl, whisk ingredients.
-Place the 4 pork chops in a large zip top bag, and pour the marinade into the bag.
-Seal the bag, and place in the refrigerator to marinate for 1-2 hours. Be sure to flip the bag halfway through the marinating time.
-Preheat your grill to medium high.
-Prepare the jicama salad by mixing the jicama, cilantro, and lime in a bowl. Set aside.
-Grill the chops for 2 ½ minutes, rotate 45 degrees and grill for another 2 ½ minutes.
-Flip and grill for another 4-6 minutes or until the internal temperature is 145-150 degrees. This will make the chops just under well done, and juicy.
-Let the chops rest for 5 minutes.
-Serve the chops with a side of the jicama salad.
-Enjoy!

Garlic and Vegetable Pork Roulade

There are three main ingredients that I find perfectly complement pork: garlic, apples, and whole grain mustard. In this dish I tried to subtly incorporate all of those great flavors into making the ultimate pork roulade.

Ingredient	Amount
Flavor Paste	-
Paprika	1 Teaspoon
Fresh Rosemary	2 Tablespoons- Finely Minced
Whole Grain Mustard	2 Teaspoons
Olive Oil	2 Tablespoons
Kosher Salt	1 Teaspoon
Black Pepper	1 Teaspoon- Ground
Roulade Filling	-
Garlic	4 Cloves- Sliced
Frozen, Chopped Spinach	1 Package- Thawed
Zucchini	1 Cup- Sliced
Apple	¾ Cup- Sliced
Butter	2 Tablespoons
Kosher Salt	½ Teaspoon
Pork Tenderloin	1 ½ Pounds

Directions

-Prepare *mise en place.*

-Thaw the frozen spinach and drain excess water by using your fingers to squeeze the water out of the spinach.

-Heat a medium skillet over a medium heat, melt the butter and sauté the garlic, add thawed spinach, zucchini, apple, and kosher salt. Sauté for 6 minutes.

-Move the sautéed ingredients into a food processor and pulse until you get the mixture to the consistency of slightly chunky peanut butter.

-Place the pork tenderloin on a cutting board and cut to one flat piece: Using the tip of a sharp knife, insert the knife about ¼ inch into the bottom corner of the tenderloin, and gently slide the knife long ways across the tenderloin. You will need to repeat this step several times until the pork lies like a flat sheet on the cutting board. If the pork is thicker than ½ inch when it is laid out, you will need to cover it with plastic wrap, and lightly flatten it with either a mallet or small skillet to thin the pork out to a ½ inch thick sheet.

-Once you have the pork laid out on the cutting board, scoop the roulade mixture on top, and evenly spread it on top of the sheet of pork.

-Using your hands, firmly grasp two corners of the sheet of pork. Tightly roll it until you form the sheet into a log shape.

-Insert 5 toothpicks, one at a time, through the pork log at a slight angle to hold the roll closed. Be sure to start at the hanging flap at the end of the pork log and push through the other side.

-In a small bowl combine the paprika, minced rosemary, mustard, olive oil, kosher salt, and black pepper. Mix to create a paste.

-Scoop the paste onto the pork log, and use your hands to spread it evenly on the entire pork log.

-Place the pork log onto a cleaned and oiled grill grate with the pork log running perpendicular to the grill grates. You may cook this on the outdoor grill, or on an indoor grill pan.

-Close the grill and let it cook for 3 minutes before flipping it ¼ turn. Repeat this step 3 more times or until all 4 sides of the pork roulade has been slightly charred.

-Move the roulade to an area of the grill where there is no contact with direct heat, this could be an area such as the upper warming rack of your grill or off to the side of your grill. Close the lid and let the pork log cook indirectly on the grill for another 3-10 minutes or until you have reached an internal temperature of 150° F

*If you cooked the pork inside on a grill pan, you will need to move the pork into a 400°F oven for the second half of the cooking process.

-Remove the pork roulade from the grill (or the oven) and cover with foil, let it rest for 5 minutes before carving.

-You may slice the pork to your desired thickness, but I recommend from ½-1 inch thick. (Remember to remove the toothpicks before carving.)

-Enjoy!

Helpful Hints

-Instead of toothpicks, you may use butchers twine to tie the pork roulade together prior to cooking.

-If you are a big garlic lover like me, you may add 2 finely minced cloves to the paste before rubbing it on the pork roulade.

-I like to drizzle the top of the slices with olive oil prior to serving.

Seafood

Shrimp Ceviche

Oh my... This is by far my favorite recipe in this book. I know I talk about my favorite recipe more than once but I can't help myself, I love good food and this is delicious. The flavors are perfectly balanced, the way the acid of the lemon compliments the shrimp is one of a kind, and when the freshness of the red onion and cilantro kicks in... ahhh please excuse me, I'm going to make myself some shrimp ceviche. I advise you do as well.

Ingredient	Amount
Shrimp Ceviche	-
Pre-Cooked Shrimp Meat	½ Pound- Peeled & Cut To Small Chunks
Lemon	Juice of 2
Lime	Juice of 1
Red Onion	¼ Cup- Finely Minced
Cilantro	2 Tablespoons- Finely Minced
Kosher Salt	¼ Teaspoon
Black Pepper	¼ Teaspoon- Ground
Accompaniment	-
Corn Chips	½ Pound Bag

Directions

-Prepare *mise en place*.
-In a bowl, combine the shrimp meat, lemon, lime, kosher salt, and black pepper, mix.
-Cover with plastic wrap and let the mixture marinate in the refrigerator for 30 minutes. (Mix half way through the marinating time.)
-Remove from the refrigerator and mix in the red onion and cilantro.
-Plate the ceviche in a small bowl and serve next to a bed of tortilla chips.
-Enjoy!

Paprika Shrimp

Shrimp is by far my favorite food so it means a lot when I say this dish is great. The shrimp are perfectly seasoned with pungent hints of rosemary, garlic, and lemon. For a unique twist on salad, try placing these grilled shrimp on top of fresh greens.

Ingredient	Amount
Paprika Shrimp	-
Rosemary Skewer	4 Firm skewers ~8 inches long (Leaves Removed)
Fresh Rosemary Leaves	2 Tablespoons- Roughly Chopped
Garlic	4 Cloves- Finely Minced
Paprika	1 Teaspoon
Olive Oil	2 Tablespoons
Kosher Salt	½ Teaspoon
Black Pepper	½ Teaspoon- Ground
Large Shrimp	1 ½ Pounds- Cleaned & Deveined
Lemon	1 Lemon- Cut to 4 wedges

Directions

-Prepare *mise en place.*
- Preheat your grill to high. (using either an outdoor grill or an indoor grill pan)
-In a large bowl thoroughly mix the rosemary leaves, garlic, paprika, olive oil, kosher salt, and black pepper.
-Place the shrimp in the bowl and mix to ensure even coating of the dressing on all of the shrimp.
-Let the shrimp sit in the dressing for 10 minutes.
-Skewer all of the shrimp on the rosemary skewers.
-Place on the grill and cook for 2 minutes.
-Flip and let cook for another 1-2 minutes or until the internal temperature has reached 140 degrees. Plate with lemon wedges.
-Enjoy!

Lemon Marinated and Panko Crusted Shrimp

This dish was originally written to be accompanied by a cream sauce, but the second I tried the shrimp by themselves, I knew they were so flavorful and delicious that they only needed to stand alone. The benefit for you? An easier recipe! (And great shrimp of course.)

Ingredient	Amount
Lemon Marinade	-
Lemon	Juice of 2 & Zest of 1
Vodka	1 Tablespoon
Garlic	3 Cloves- Finely Minced
Large Shrimp	1 ½ Pounds- Cleaned & Deveined
Panko Dredge	-
Panko Bread Crumbs	1 Cup
Parsley	1 Tablespoon- Finely Chopped
Lemon	Zest of 1 Lemon
Kosher Salt	¼ Teaspoon
Black Pepper	½ Teaspoon
Vegetable/Canola Oil	2 Teaspoons

Directions

-Prepare *mise en place.*
-In a large zip top plastic bag combine the marinade: lemon juice, lemon zest, vodka, garlic, and shrimp.
-Let marinate for 30 minutes in the refrigerator. Be sure to flip the bag over halfway through the marinating time.
-In a medium mixing bowl combine the panko, parsley, lemon zest, kosher salt, and black pepper. Mix the ingredients thoroughly and set aside.
-Spread the oil evenly around a large roasting pan or sheet pan.
-Preheat your oven to 425 degrees.
-Remove the shrimp from the refrigerator and one at a time place in the panko mixture. Use your hands to pack on the mixture so it doesn't fall off.
-After you have crusted the shrimp, place them on the oiled roasting/sheet pan. Make sure that none of the shrimp overlap.
-Place in the oven for 6-8 minutes or until the tops are golden brown and the internal temperature has reached 140 degrees. I recommend serving with a wedge of lemon.
-Enjoy!

Summer Citrus Mahi Mahi, Swordfish, or Shrimp

I am a die hard fan of having fresh herbs and citrus on my seafood, so I took it upon myself to make what I think is the ultimate seafood marinade. This dish can be made with any of the types of fish in the title. The dish is refreshing and flavorful, and has a nice little spice.

Ingredient	Amount
Marinade	-
Lemon	Juice & Zest of 1
Lime	Juice & Zest of 1
Orange	Juice & Zest of 1
Olive Oil	2 Tablespoons
Fresh Rosemary	2 Tablespoons- Roughly Chopped
Fresh Cilantro	2 Tablespoons- Roughly Chopped
Crushed Red Pepper Flakes	¼ Teaspoon
Kosher Salt	¼ Teaspoon
Black Pepper	½ Teaspoon- Ground
Mahi, Swordfish, or Shrimp	1 ½ Pounds

Directions

-Prepare *mise en place.*
-In a large plastic zip top bag, combine the lemon juice and zest, lime juice and zest, orange juice and zest, olive oil, rosemary, cilantro, red pepper flakes, kosher salt, black pepper, and your chosen seafood.
-Let the fish marinade in the refrigerator for 30 minutes. Be sure to flip the bag halfway through the marinating time.
-Preheat your grill. For shrimp, preheat to high, and cook for 2 minutes, flip and cook for 1-2 more minutes on the second side. For mahi mahi and swordfish, preheat your grill to medium high, and cook the fish for 3-4 minutes per side or until the internal temperature has reached 140 degrees.
-Enjoy!

Pan Seared Halibut with a Baby Spinach and Shaved Parmesan Salad

I usually go by the rule that seafood should not be prepared with cheese, but after the first time I tested this recipe I knew that this would be the exception. The parmesan provides texture as well as delivering a nice salty bite to the salad. Enjoy!

Ingredient	Amount
Spice Rub	-
Dried Thyme	2 Teaspoons- Ground
Paprika	1 Teaspoon- Ground
Cumin	1 Teaspoon- Ground
Onion Powder	1 Teaspoon- Ground
Garlic	2 Cloves- Finely Minced
Kosher Salt	¼ Teaspoon
Black Pepper	½ Teaspoon- Ground
Olive Oil	2 Tablespoons
Spinach Salad	-
Baby Spinach	Handful Per Plate
Parmesan	1 Tablespoon- Shaved
Dressing	-
Olive Oil	1/3 Cup
Lemon	Juice & Zest of 1
Dried or Fresh Rosemary	2 Teaspoons
Red Wine Vinegar	2 Tablespoons
Halibut Filets	1 ½ Pounds- Cut to 4 Filets

Directions

-Prepare *mise en place.*
-Combine the dressing: olive oil, lemon juice and zest, rosemary, and red wine vinegar in a bowl, set aside to let the flavours infuse.
-Rub a portion of the minced garlic onto each piece of fish.
 -In a small bowl mix the thyme, paprika, cumin, onion powder, kosher salt, and pepper.
-Put the spice rub into an empty spice shaker or use a spoon to evenly apply the spice rub to all sides of the halibut.
-Prepare a plate for each serving with a handful of spinach and shaved parmesan, set aside.
-Heat a large skillet over medium heat and pour the olive oil into the pan.
-Place the seasoned halibut filets in the pan and cook for 3-4 minutes. (You should leave them undisturbed to form a crispy crust.)
- Flip the halibut filets over and cook for another 2-4 minutes, or until the internal temperature of the fish reaches 140 degrees.
-Strain the rosemary from the dressing, whisk the dressing to combine, and ladle about 2 tablespoons of dressing onto each spinach salad.
-Plate the halibut filets on top of the spinach salads.
-Enjoy!

Helpful Hints

-To ensure a crispy crust, pat the halibut filets with paper towels until dry prior to applying the spice rub.
-The easiest way to create shavings of parmesan is to use a vegetable peeler. I prefer shaved cheese over shredded on the baby spinach salad because of the unique texture it gives to the dish.

Mediterranean Spice Encrusted Halibut

A flavorful and easy way to cook halibut (as well as other similar white fish) is to create a nice spice and herb rub for the fish, and cook it over the grill, under the broiler, or in a pan to yield a 'blackened' crust. This recipe has a great balance of flavors, complimenting the fish in a very delicious way.

Ingredient	Amount
Spice Rub	-
Paprika	½ Teaspoon
Dried Oregano	1 Teaspoon
Dried Thyme	½ Teaspoon
Coriander	½ Teaspoon- Ground
Cumin	½ Teaspoon
Black Pepper	½ Teaspoon- Ground
Kosher Salt	½ Teaspoon
Halibut Filets	1 ½ Pounds- Cut to 4 Filets

Directions

-Prepare *mise en place.*
-Preheat your grill to medium high.
-In a small bowl combine the paprika, oregano, thyme, coriander, cumin, black pepper, and kosher salt.
-Evenly spread the rub over all sides of the halibut filets.
-Place the fish on the clean and oiled grill grates and cook for 4 minutes.
-Flip and cook for another 2-4 minutes or until the internal temperature has reached 140 degrees.
-Enjoy!

Potato and Macadamia Crusted Halibut

This recipe pushes the extremes when it comes to playing with different textures in a dish. By using dried potato flakes (normally used to make instant mashed potato) we are able to create what I would say is the best crust I have ever seen on fish. Add on the crunch of finely minced macadamia nuts and then top with the tasty tomato basil relish, we get a delicious and unique combination of flavors and well as textures.

Ingredient	Amount
Crusted Halibut	-
Dried Potato Flakes	½ Cup
Macadamia Nuts	½ Cup- Finely Minced
Kosher Salt	¼ Teaspoon
Black Pepper	½ Teaspoon- Ground
Vegetable Oil	1 Tablespoon
Halibut Filet	1 ½ Pounds- Cut to 4 Filets
Tomato Basil Relish	-
Tomato Basil Relish	1 Recipe on Page 125

Directions

-Prepare *mise en place.*
-Mix the dried potato flakes and the finely minced macadamia nuts.
-Pour the mixture onto a plate.
-Sprinkle the halibut filets with kosher salt and black pepper.
-Evenly coat all sides of the filets in the potato and nut mixture. Use your hand to pack the mixture onto each filet.
-Prepare the Tomato Basil Relish according to the directions on page 125.
-Preheat a pan to medium heat and pour the oil into the pan.
-Place the filets into the pan and cook for 4 minutes.
-Flip and cook for another 3-4 minutes, or until the internal temperature has reached 140 degrees.
-Plate the fish with the tomato basil relish.
-Enjoy!

Maple and Citrus Salmon

Years ago at one of grandma's parties, the salmon that was served for dinner had an extremely unique sweetness to it. I asked the caterer what was on it and I was very surprised to hear 'maple syrup' come out of his mouth. Though the ingredients may surprise you, the maple syrup provides a subtle and unmatched sweetness to this recipe.

Ingredient	Amount
Marinade	-
Lemon	Juice & Zest of 1
Orange	Juice & Zest of 1
Vegetable/Canola Oil	1 Tablespoon
Kosher Salt	¼ Teaspoon
Black Pepper	½ Teaspoon- Ground
Salmon Filet	1 ½ Pounds- Cut to 4 Filets
Glaze	-
Maple Syrup	¼ Cup
Lemon	Juice & Zest of 1
Orange	Juice & Zest of 1

Directions

-Prepare *mise en place.*
-In a large plastic zip top bag combine the marinade: lemon juice and zest, orange juice and zest, oil, kosher salt, black pepper and salmon filets. Move to refrigerator.
-Let the salmon marinate for 30 minutes.
-Preheat your oven to 425 degrees.
-Place the salmon on an oiled glass casserole dish.
-Place in the oven for 14-16 minutes or until the internal temperature has reached 140 degrees.
-While the salmon is in the oven whisk together the glaze: maple syrup, lemon juice and zest, and the orange juice and zest.
-Pour the maple and citrus glaze over the baked salmon.
-Enjoy!

Baked Salmon with Dill Compound Butter

The first few years of my culinary career were spent experimenting with different flavors to see what went well together. One of the combinations that I really liked was salmon and dill. This dish is distinct yet mellow, and provides a great fresh taste. It is fast, easy, healthy and delicious.

Ingredient	Amount
Salmon	-
Fresh Dill	2 Teaspoons- Finely Chopped
Olive Oil	2 Teaspoons
Lemon	Juice of ½ Lemon
Kosher Salt	¼ Teaspoon
Black Pepper	¼ Teaspoon- Ground
Salmon	1 ½ Pounds- Filet
Dill Compound Butter	-
Butter	3 Tablespoons- Softened
Dill	1 Teaspoon- Finely Chopped

Directions

-Prepare *mise en place.*
-Preheat your oven to 375 degrees.
-In a small bowl combine the softened butter with the 1 teaspoon of dill. Mix thoroughly and place the mixture on a sheet of wax paper.
-Roll the wax paper into a log and place into the freezer.
-Place the dill, kosher salt, and black pepper on the salmon.
-Place half of the olive oil in a large casserole dish and evenly spread around the dish.
-Place the salmon in the oiled casserole dish.
-Bake for 17-23 minutes or until you have reached an internal temperature of 140 degrees.
-Remove the salmon from the oven and pour the lemon juice and remaining olive oil over the salmon.
-Remove the compound butter log from the freezer, cut a few slices off and place them over the baked salmon.
-Enjoy!

Rice

Wild Rice Stuffed Chile with Broiled Romano

These stuffed peppers are like a healthy, inside-out chile rellano remix. I prefer using the wild rice and brown rice in this dish because it adds a little nuttiness and texture. This recipe is great because it can be prepared ahead of time and finished last minute.

Ingredient	Amount
Rice Filling	-
Onion	¼ Medium Onion- Finely Diced
Garlic	2 Cloves- Finely Minced
Cilantro	2 Tablespoons- Finely Chopped
Olive Oil	2 Teaspoons
Wild Rice	½ Cup
Brown Rice	½ Cup
Vegetable Stock	2 Cups
Kosher Salt	¼ Teaspoon
White Pepper	¼ Teaspoon- Ground
Chile	-
Poblano	4 Chile Peppers
Romano Cheese	1/3 Cup- Shredded

Directions

-Prepare *mise en place.*
-Blister the skin of the chilies either on the grill, over a gas burner, or under a broiler.
-After the chile skins are blistered place them immediately into a large plastic zip top bag. Seal the bag and let the chilies sit for 5 minutes. (placing them in the bag after blistering the skins should help the skins come right off)
-Using your fingers, rub the skins off of the chilies.
-Place a medium saucepot over medium heat. Pour the olive oil in.
-Cook the onions in the oil until they become translucent (about 4-5 minutes). Add the garlic, kosher salt, and black pepper. Let cook for 1 more minute.
-Stir both types of rice into the garlic and onion mixture. Continue to cook the rice for 1 minute.
-Pour in the vegetable stock and bring to a boil over high heat.
-Reduce the heat to low, cover, and cook until all of the water has evaporated and the rice is tender. (about 25-30 minutes)
-When the rice has finished cooking, mix in the cilantro.
-Preheat your broiler to high.
-Using a knife, make a slit than runs the entire length of the top of the skinless chile.
-Separate the opening on the chile, carefully remove the seeds, and then stuff the chile with the rice mixture. Repeat on the last 3 chilies.
-Sprinkle the top with the romano cheese, place on an oven safe tray, and place under the broiler for 2-3 minutes or until the cheese is golden brown.
-Enjoy!

Citrus Rice with Fresh Herbs

This recipe is incredibly simple, yet the end result is a dish that has distinct and refreshing flavor. Citrus Rice is so tasty that it can be addicting as a snack or used as a versatile side dish that perfectly complements a meal, especially blackened or grilled chicken or fish.

Ingredient	Amount
Citrus Rice	-
Long Grain Rice	1 ½ Cups
Olive Oil	2 Tablespoons
Water	2 ¾ Cups
Butter	2 Tablespoons- Softened
Lemon	Juice of ½ Lemon
Lime	Juice of ½ Lime
Orange	Juice of ½ Orange
Fresh Flat Leaf Parsley	2 Tablespoons- Finely Minced
Kosher Salt	½ Teaspoon
Black Pepper	¼ Teaspoon- Ground

Directions

-Prepare *mise en place.*
-Heat a medium sauce pot over a medium high heat.
-Pour in the olive oil and the rice.
-Toast the rice for 3-5 minutes stirring frequently.
-Remove the pot from the heat and let it cool for 2 minutes.
-Pour in the water, and butter. Stir, and move the pot back to a low heat.
-Cover and simmer for 15-20 minutes or until all of the water is absorbed and the rice is tender.
-While the rice is cooking, extract all of the juice from the lemon, lime, and orange.
-Turn off the heat; thoroughly mix in all of the juice from the citrus, and the finely minced parsley.
-You may serve in the pot, or move to a decorative bowl and garnish with a slice (or 3) of citrus and a sprig of parsley.
-Enjoy!

Helpful Hints

-The reason for briefly removing the pot from the heat is to let the rice slightly cool down to help reduce splattering when adding water. Since the pot and the rice get so hot during the toasting process, you need to be careful while pouring in the water. Always use caution and avoid an unexpected and unwanted facial of hot steam and jumping water droplets while cooking.

Fried Rice with Garlic Butter

Fried rice was the first very successful dish that I had ever created and cooked on my own. It became my hobby as a child to go in the kitchen and make fried rice. I remember that in the 4th grade I brought a rice cooker and griddle into class and put on a "How to Make Fried Rice" demonstration for the rest of the kids in class. Of course in between 4th grade and now I learned a few tricks that added to the deliciousness of the fried rice. So here you go... The perfected version of my first successful creation.

Ingredient	Amount
Rice	-
Short Grain Rice	2 Cups
Water	3 ¼ Cups
Stir Fried Mix Ins	-
Onion	½ Cup- Chopped
Carrot	½ Cup- Chopped
Zucchini	½ Cup- Chopped
Button Mushroom	½ Cup- Chopped
Scallion	1 Tablespoon- Thinly Sliced
Eggs	3- Scrambled
Vegetable/Canola Oil	2 Tablespoons
Soy Sauce	2 Tablespoons
Sesame Oil	1 Teaspoon
Black Pepper	½ Teaspoon- Ground
Garlic Butter	-
Butter	2 Tablespoons- Softened
Garlic	2 Cloves- Finely Minced

Directions

-Prepare *mise en place.*
-In a large saucepot bring the water to a boil.
-Add the rice, reduce heat to low, and cover.
-Cook until all of the water has been absorbed and the rice is tender (about 17-22 minutes)
-Remove the rice from the heat, uncover, and let sit for 10 minutes to cool down.
-Place a large frying pan over medium-high heat. (a wok would be great if you have one)
-Pour in the vegetable/canola oil.
-Add the onions, carrot, and zucchini and cook until they are tender (about 3 minutes). Add the mushrooms and cook for another minute.
-Remove the veggies from the pan. Add the eggs to the pan and scramble until they are cooked, and chopped into small bites.
-Return the veggies back to the heat.
-Dump the rice into the pan of ingredients, add the scallions and cook until the rice is hot. Stir frequently to thoroughly mix all of the ingredients.
-In a small bowl thoroughly mix the softened butter and the garlic.
-After the rice is hot, mix in the pepper, soy sauce, sesame oil, and garlic butter. Mix thoroughly and remove from the heat.
-Enjoy!

Seared Sticky Rice Cakes with Soy Drizzle

Looking for something different to serve with dinner? Or possibly just looking for a new snack? Seared Sticky Rice Cakes are a great option. Cook them in a bit of oil to create a satisfying crispy treat and then top with a little soy sauce. If you are craving comfort food but don't want the guilty feeling that comes with it, try this version of my favorite snack. These crispy rice cakes with soy drizzle prove to be a delicious and satisfying savory treat.

Ingredient	Amount
Rice	-
Short Grain/ Sushi Rice	1 ½ Cups
Water	2 ½ Cups
Vegetable Oil	2 Tablespoons
Soy Sauce	Light Drizzle Over Each Cake
Roasted Sesame Seeds	1 Teaspoon

Directions

-Prepare *mise en place*.
-In a large saucepot bring the water to a boil.
-Add the rice, reduce heat to low, and cover.
-Cook until all of the water has been absorbed and the rice is tender (about 17-22 minutes)
-Remove the rice from the heat, uncover, and let sit for 15 minutes to cool down.
-Fluff the rice with a fork and let it sit for another 10 minutes to continue cooling.
-Slightly wet your hands, grab a handful of rice, and gently pat it into an even disk shaped rice cake that is about ¾ inch thick (use about ½ cup of cooked rice per cake)
-After all of the cakes have been formed, place a large frying pan over medium high heat.
-Add the vegetable oil and evenly distribute the oil throughout the pan.
-Place the rice cakes into the pan and cook for 3-4 minutes or until they are golden brown on the bottom side.
-Flip and cook for another 3-4 minutes or until golden brown on the second side.
-Turn the heat off and lightly drizzle the soy sauce on each browned rice cake. Garnish the top of each rice cake with roasted sesame seeds.
-Enjoy!

Potato

Roasted Red Potato Wedges with Infused Olive Oil

Possibly as addicting as French fries, this healthy cousin to the dish delivers more flavor without the bad rap. Rosemary and thyme provide savory flavors to moist, perfectly roasted red potato wedges. This is one of the first recipes that I wrote for my cookbook and certainly one of my favorites.

Ingredient	Amount
Potatoes	-
Red Potatoes	2 Pounds- Cut to Wedges
Kosher Salt	1 Teaspoon
Black Pepper	1 Teaspoon- Ground
Infused Olive Oil	-
Olive Oil	1/3 Cup
Garlic	3 Cloves- Minced
Dried Thyme	1 Tablespoon
Dried Rosemary	2 Teaspoons

Directions

-Prepare *mise en place*.
-In a large bowl combine the olive oil, garlic, dried thyme, and dried rosemary. Thoroughly mix.
-Let the mixture sit for 15 minutes.
-Preheat the oven to 425 degrees.
-In the large bowl combine the wedged potatoes and infused olive oil mixture.
-Toss to make sure that all of the potatoes are evenly coated with the infused olive oil.
-Place the coated potatoes onto a nonstick roasting or sheet pan and evenly spread throughout the pan.
-Equally sprinkle the kosher salt and black pepper on top of the potatoes.
-Place the potatoes into the oven and let cook for about 23-27 minutes or until they are golden on the outside and have soft insides. Be sure to flip the potatoes about halfway through cooking.
-Enjoy!

Helpful Hints

-You will want to pull one potato out to test its doneness before removing the entire batch from the oven.
-Make sure you place the tray in the middle of the oven. If it is too close to the heating element, the bottoms will burn before the rest of the potato has finished cooking.

Cheesy Mashed Potatoes with Bacon Crumbles

Do I really need an intro here? The title says it all! If this flavorful mashed potato recipe sounds tempting, I'm sure it will become a regular in your kitchen.

Ingredient	Amount
Potatoes	-
Yukon Gold Potatoes	2 Pounds- Quartered
Water	2-3 Quarts- Boiling
Mix Ins	-
Butter	3 Tablespoons- Softened
Milk	1 Cup
Cheddar Cheese	1 Cup- Shredded
Parmesan Cheese	1/3 Cup- Shredded
Bacon	5 Slices- Cooked & Crumbled
Garlic	2 Cloves- Finely Minced
Kosher Salt	½ Teaspoon
Black Pepper	1 Teaspoon- Ground

Directions

-Prepare *mise en place.*
-Pour the water into a large pot and place over high heat, bring to a boil.
-Once the water has boiled, carefully place the potatoes into the water, and reduce the heat to medium.
-Let the potatoes cook for 15-23 minutes or until they are tender.
-While the potatoes are cooking, crisp the bacon according to the directions on the package. Let cool and then break into small pieces. Set aside.
-Drain the water from the potatoes and then return the pot of potatoes back to a very low heat.
-Add the butter and milk to the potatoes, and then slightly smash the mixture.
-After the potatoes are smashed into small chunks, stir in the cheddar cheese, parmesan cheese, bacon bits, garlic, kosher salt, and black pepper.
-Gently stir all of the ingredients together. (The potatoes should have finished mashing during the stirring step.) Turn off the heat.
-Enjoy!

Bread

Herb Infused Focaccia

"Calling all freshly baked bread lovers… Eat this one warm from the oven."
Bake the bread into individual loaves, or roll out the dough to make an exceptional gourmet pizza crust.

Ingredient	Amount
Focaccia Dough	-
Bread Flour	3 Cups
Active Dry Yeast	1 Packet
Granulated Sugar	2 Teaspoons
Dried Rosemary	2 Teaspoons- Finely Minced
Dried Thyme	2 Teaspoons- Finely Minced
Water	1 Cup
Olive Oil	2 Tablespoons
Table Salt	½ Teaspoon
Black Pepper	½ Teaspoon- Ground
Topping	-
Romano Cheese	½ Cup- Shredded

Directions

-Prepare *mise en place*.

-Sift the flour, yeast, sugar, rosemary, thyme, salt, and pepper into the bowl of a stand mixer.

*If you do not have a stand mixer, sift into a glass bowl.

-Using the dough hook attachment, turn the stand mixer to low, and begin to slowly pour in the olive oil, and the water. If you find you need more water, you can add 1 teaspoon more at a time. Make sure you don't add too much to make the dough sticky.

*If you do not have a stand mixer, place the wet ingredients into the glass bowl, and kneed with your hands until the dough comes together.

- Remove the dough ball from the bowl, and then lightly rub the inside of the bowl with olive oil.

-Place the dough back into the oiled bowl, and cover the bowl with a moist kitchen towel.

-Move the bowl to a very warm area that has a temperature close to 100°F, like your oven or a warm spot on the counter near a window, and let the dough rise for 1 hour.

-Remove the dough from the bowl and use your hands to knead the dough for about 20 seconds. Shape the dough back into a ball.

-Move the dough back into the oiled bowl, cover with the damp towel, and place in the very warm area once again, let it rise for another hour.

-Remove the dough from the bowl, and place it on a large working area such as a very large cutting board, or a big sheet of wax/parchment paper.

-Preheat your oven to 400°F, and position an oven rack as far away from the heating element as possible.

-Use olive oil to evenly grease a large sheet pan, or large cookie sheet.

-Cut the dough into 4 even sections.

-You will need to prepare each dough section individually as follows:

> - Roll the section into a ball.
> - Place it on a lightly floured section of your work space.
> -Use the palm of your hand to slightly flatten the ball into a patty shape that is about 5 inches in diameter.
> -Use your fingers to poke about 5-10 small indentations in the top of the flattened dough patty.
> - Place the dough onto the oiled sheet pan/cookie sheet.
> -Repeat for the last 3 dough sections.

-Once you have all 4 dough sections shaped, and on the sheet pan, evenly sprinkle the top of each with the shredded Romano cheese. Feel free to substitute Parmesan for the Romano.

-Put the dough into the oven and bake for 8 minutes.

-After the 8 minutes are up, remove the sheet pan, rotate it 180°, and bake for another 8 minutes.

- After a total bake time of 16 minutes, remove from the oven, serve, and enjoy!

Helpful Hints

-The easiest way to get the spice to a fine consistency is to use a mortar and pestle, if you do not have one you can put the dried herbs into a zip-top bag, and using either a rolling pin, wine bottle, or skillet, crush the herbs to a fine consistency.

-I find the easiest warm place to let the bread rise is an oven. In order to do this, set your oven to preheat to the lowest setting and as soon as it begins to warm, shut the oven completely off, and place the bowl of dough in the oven to rise.

- Try serving Italian style by slicing the bread into wedges and serve while hot with a dip of olive oil and coarsely ground black pepper.

- You can also butterfly the focaccia and use it as sandwich bread.

-This bread dough may also be rolled out to be used as pizza dough.

Italian Breadsticks

Gather the family and bring them in the kitchen. Preparing these hand-shaped breadsticks together is just as much fun as eating them. Use the pictures for your artistic inspiration. These are delicious when eaten fresh and warm out of the oven.

Ingredient	Amount
Bread Dough	-
Bread Flour	3 ¾ Cups
Granulated Sugar	2 Teaspoons
Active Dry Yeast	1 Packet
Parmesan Cheese	½ Cup + ¼ Cup- Shredded
Garlic Powder	½ Teaspoon
Onion Powder	1 Teaspoon
Kosher Salt	½ Teaspoon
Fresh Parsley	2 Tablespoons- Finely Minced
Olive Oil	2 Tablespoons
Melted Butter	4 Tablespoons
Milk	1 Cup

Directions

-Prepare *mise en place*.
-In a large bowl combine the bread flour, sugar, yeast, ½ cup parmesan, garlic powder, onion powder, and kosher salt. Thoroughly mix together all of the dry ingredients.
-In a separate bowl mix the parsley, olive oil, milk and melted butter together.
-Pour the wet ingredients into the bowl of dry ingredients.
-Use the dough hook attachment on your stand mixer (or your hands if you do not have a stand mixer) to knead the dough for 3 minutes.
-Place a moist towel over the bowl of dough and let rise in a warm area for 1 hour.
-Pour the dough out onto a large cutting board and using a rolling pin, roll the dough out to a thickness of ¼ inch.
-Preheat your oven to 375 degrees.
-Feel free to cut and shape the dough however you would like, they can be as simple or as complex as you would like. (Use the pictures of the recipe for some examples on ways you could shape the dough.)
-Place the shaped bread dough onto a nonstick sheet pan or cookie sheet and sprinkle the top with ¼ cup of parmesan. Bake for 10-15 minutes or until the tops are golden brown.
 -Enjoy

Aryei

ORGAN

Bosc Pear

$2.99lb

94413

FARM

Dessert

Poached Pears

Although the title might sound a little intimidating for some, this dish is quite simple and easy to make. These poached pears are classic, sweet and something that will leave your guests raving.

Ingredient	Amount
Poaching Liquid	-
Red Wine	4 Cups
Water	3 Cups
Brown Sugar	¾ Cup
Cinnamon Sticks	2 Sticks- Each About 4 Inches Long
Orange Peel	Peel From ½ Orange
Pears	4- Skins Peeled Off
Vanilla Ice Cream	4 Scoops- About 2 Cups Total

Directions

-Prepare *mise en place.*
-In a large pot combine the red wine, water, brown sugar, cinnamon, and orange peel.
-Bring to a simmer over medium heat.
-Peel the skin off of the pears. Be sure to leave the stems intact.
-Place the pears in the simmering liquid and reduce the heat to low. Cook for 40 minutes stirring occasionally.
-Remove pears from the liquid and place on a plate to let cool for 10 minutes.
-Meanwhile turn the heat to medium high and reduce the liquid to half of the original volume.
-Serve the pears alongside vanilla ice cream and the reduced simmering liquid.
-Enjoy!

Strawberry Cheesecake

I think there is a scientist in me that comes out when I start working in the kitchen. I enjoy seeing a dessert being made from scratch, and I get personal fulfillment from taking individual ingredients, mixing them together and creating an entire dish. This soft, moist cheesecake recipe is certain to satisfy the cheesecake lover's craving. The fresh strawberry coulis provides a great flavor and really makes this dish pop.

Ingredient	Amount
Filling	-
Granulated Sugar	½ Cup
Butter	½ Cup- Softened
Eggs	3
Cream Cheese	3- 8 Ounce Packs- Softened
Lemon Juice	2 Tablespoons
Vanilla Extract	1 Teaspoon
Strawberry Coulis	-
Strawberry	1 ½ Cups- Sliced
Lemon Juice	2 Tablespoons
Granulated Sugar	¼ Cup
Graham Cracker Crust	-
Graham Crackers	1 ¾ Cups- Ground
Butter	½ Cup- Melted
Granulated Sugar	¼ Cup
Honey	1 Teaspoon

Directions

-Prepare *mise en place.*

-Preheat your oven to 350 degrees.

-In a medium sauce pot over medium heat combine the sliced strawberries, lemon juice, and sugar. Stir occasionally and cook for 15 minutes or until the mixture resembles a thick syrup.

-Purée the strawberry mixture until it is a silky texture.

-While the strawberries are cooking, pulse the graham crackers in your food processor until the mixture becomes almost sand-like. If you do not have a food processor, you can finely crumble the graham crackers by hand.

-Pour in the butter, sugar, and honey into the ground graham crackers. Pulse again until the mixture is thoroughly combined.

-Scoop the crust mixture into a cheesecake pan (you may use a large pie pan) and use your fingers to evenly spread and pack the mixture throughout the bottom and walls of the pan.

-Place the crust into the oven for 6 minutes. Remove and place on the counter to cool.

-While the crust is cooling, turn your stand mixer onto medium and beat the sugar, and butter until the mixture begins to blend and lighten in color. (About 1-2 minutes) Add the eggs one at a time. Don't add the next egg until the previous yolk has completely mixed into the mixture.

-After all eggs are mixed in, add the softened cream cheese packs one at a time, and once again wait until the previous installment is completely integrated before adding the next pack.

-Pour the cheesecake mixture into the crust and evenly spread.

-Place the cheesecake into the oven for 35 minutes on a water bath. (To create a water bath, place the cheesecake pan onto a larger pan, such as a roast pan, with ½ inch of water in it).

-Lightly drizzle the puréed strawberry coulis on top of the cheesecake and place back into the 350 degree oven for 15-25 more minutes or until the center has just set. Save any extra strawberry sauce to garnish each piece of cheesecake when serving.

-Cool in the refrigerator for 4-6 hours before serving.

-Enjoy!

Sauce & Garnish

Marinara with a Kick

A great marinara sauce is one of the most versatile things in the kitchen. This rendition of the classic Italian staple offers a blend of fresh produce and herbs. The "with a kick' title is your disclaimer about the spice; cut back on the red pepper flakes if you prefer a milder marinara. This recipe can be placed on anything from bread to pasta to different meats. Try making a double batch of the sauce, it stores nicely in the freezer for future uses.

Ingredient	Amount
Marinara	-
Tomato	3 Pounds
Olive Oil	¼ Cup
Onion	¼ Medium Onion- Finely Diced
Garlic	2 Cloves- Finely Minced
Red Pepper Flake	1/8 Teaspoon
Dried Oregano	1 Teaspoon
Dried Basil	1 Teaspoon
Bay Leaf	1 Leaf
Granulated Sugar	1 Teaspoon
Fresh Basil	¼ Cup Thinly sliced
Fresh Parsley	2 Teaspoons- Finely Chopped
Kosher Salt	½ Teaspoon
Black Pepper	½ Teaspoon- Ground

Directions

-Prepare mise en place.
-Cut a small "X" on the top of every tomato.
-Place the tomatoes in a pot of boiling water for 30 seconds, and then transfer the tomatoes to a bowl of ice water for 1 minute. (Putting them into hot water, and then directly into ice water, known as blanching and shocking, will help you peel the skins off easily.)
-Peel the skin off the tomatoes using your fingers.
-Finely dice all of the tomatoes.
-Place a large pot over medium heat.
-Add the olive oil, onion, red pepper flakes, and kosher salt. Cook the onions for about 4-5 minutes or until they begin to turn translucent. Stir occasionally.
-Add the minced garlic and cook for another minute.
-Pour in the diced tomatoes, dried oregano, dried basil, bay leaf, sugar, and black pepper.
-Bring to a gentle boil and let cook for 10 minutes, stirring occasionally.
-Reduce heat to medium-low.
-Use a hand blender to purée the marinara into a smooth sauce. (You can also pour the mixture into a regular blender and than return to the pot after it is puréed.)
-Simmer for 30 minutes. Be sure to stir every 5-10 minutes.
 -Turn off the heat.
-Pour in the fresh basil and fresh parsley. Stir thoroughly.
-Enjoy!

Helpful Hints

-For a simple and quick pasta recipe, boil and drain pasta and then top with this delicious sauce. If you want to change it up, you can pour the pasta and sauce mixture into a casserole dish, top with shredded parmesan cheese, or layer parmesan and other cheese in the pasta. Place casserole dish under the broiler until the top is golden brown.

Tomato Basil Relish

This simple tomato dish only takes about 10 minutes to make from start to finish. It is extremely versatile and can be placed on anything from fish or chicken to toasted French bread or chips. Also try just eating it as a delicious tomato salad, by itself for a healthy snack.

Ingredient	Amount
Tomato Basil Relish	-
Tomato	1 ½ Cups- Diced
Basil	2 Tablespoons-Thinly Sliced
Garlic	1 Clove-Finely Minced
Olive Oil	2 Teaspoons
Balsamic Vinegar	½ Teaspoon
Kosher Salt	½ Teaspoon
Black pepper	½ Teaspoon-Ground

Directions

-Prepare *mise en place.*
-In a medium bowl combine the tomato, basil, garlic, olive oil, balsamic vinegar, kosher salt, and black pepper.
-Thoroughly mix to combine all ingredients.
-Enjoy!

Modern Basil Pesto

Traditional pesto is delicious, but I think that adding a little bit of cilantro and almonds provides a unique new twist to this classic sauce. It can be placed on fish, potatoes, pasta, chicken, and just about anything else that you are adventurous enough to try with this bold, nutty and addictive pesto.

Ingredient	Amount
Pesto	-
Basil	2 Cups- Whole Leaves
Cilantro	1 Cup- Whole leaves
Parmesan Cheese	1/3 Cup- Shredded
Roasted Almonds	1/3 Cup
Garlic	2 Cloves- Peeled
Olive Oil	1/3 Cup
Kosher Salt	1 Teaspoon
Black Pepper	½ Teaspoon- Ground

Directions

-Prepare *mise en place.*
-In a food processor pulse the garlic, and roasted almonds until they are finely minced.
-Add the basil, cilantro, parmesan cheese, olive oil, kosher salt, and black pepper.
-Pulse again until the mixture forms into a smooth paste.
You may want to scrape down the sides of the bowl to make sure that all ingredients have been blended.
-Enjoy!

Index

Salad & Dressing

Lemon Rosemary Vinaigrette – 31
Rosemary and garlic infused olive oil mixed with fresh lemon

Whole Grain Mustard Vinaigrette - 33
A savory blend of whole grain mustard, fresh herbs, and olive oil

Beef

Charbroiled Rib Eye – 37
Simply marinated rib eye, grilled over a hot charcoal grill

New York Burgers with Parmesan Frico – 39
Freshly ground steak with flavorful mix-ins and a parmesan "cracker"

Grilled Beef Skewers – 41
Beef skewers saturated in a fresh Asian inspired marinade.

Chicken

Brined Chicken Breast with Modern Basil Pesto – 45
Chicken breast marinated in a slightly salty brine and finished with fresh modern basil pesto

Chicken Dumplings with Citrus Soy Glaze – 47
Pan seared and steamed chicken dumplings paired with a flavorful dipping sauce

Lemon Chicken Breast with Heirloom Tomato & Baby Spinach Salad – 49
Marinated chicken breast placed on top of baby spinach and tomatoes with a light vinaigrette

Chicken Picatta – 53
A flavorful rendition of a classic chicken dish simmered in a lemon, garlic, and caper sauce

Tuscan Flared Roasted Chicken – 55
A whole flattened and roasted chicken with a Tuscan inspired herb paste

Mustard Glazed Pork Chop with Jicama Salad – 59
A boneless pork chop marinated in mustard and lime juice finished with a light jicama salad

Garlic and Vegetable Pork Roulade – 61
Stuffed pork tenderloin with a flavorful herb and spice paste, grilled, and sliced

Shrimp Ceviche – 67
Succulent shrimp meat marinated in citrus, red onion, and cilantro served alongside corn tortilla chips

Paprika Shrimp – 69
Shrimp marinated in a flavorful combination of paprika, rosemary, olive oil, and garlic, grilled on rosemary skewers

Lemon Marinated and Panko Crusted Shrimp – 71
Baked lemony shrimp lightly dusted with spiced panko breadcrumbs

Summer Citrus Mahi Mahi, Swordfish, or Shrimp – 73
A light and flavorful citrus marinade that compliments your choice of 3 sea foods

Pan Seared Halibut with a Baby Spinach and Shaved Parmesan Salad – 75
Spice encrusted halibut on a flavorful spinah salad

Mediterranean Spice Encrusted Halibut – 79
Grilled halibut encrusted in a perfect mix of Mediterranean herbs and spices

Potato and Macadamia Crusted Halibut – 81
Crusted pan seared halibut finished with a side of tomato basil relish

Maple and Citrus Salmon – 83
Citrus marinated salmon finished with a slightly sweet citrus maple glaze

Baked Salmon with Dill Compound Butter – 85
Simply baked salmon topped with fresh dill compound butter

Wild Rice Stuffed Chile with Broiled Romano – 89
Roasted poblano chile stuffed with a wild rice and herb mixture finished with broiled romano cheese

Citrus Rice with Fresh Herbs – 91
Toasted and steamed basmati rice finished with citrus and parsley

Fried Rice with Garlic Butter – 93
Stir fried rice mixed with vegetables, soy, sesame, and fresh garlic butter

Seared Sticky Rice Cakes with Soy Drizzle – 95
Crispy pan seared rice cakes drizzled with soy sauce and sesame seeds

Potato

Roasted Red Potato Wedges with Infused Olive Oil – 99
Red potato wedges mixed with flavorful infused olive oil and roasted in a hot oven

Cheesy Mashed Potatoes with Bacon Crumbles – 101
A flavorful rendition of classic mashed potatoes

Bread

Herb Infused Focaccia – 105
Freshly made focaccia bread with the pungent flavors of rosemary and thyme

Italian Breadsticks - 109
Flavorful fresh breadsticks with parsley and parmesan

Dessert

Poached Pears – 113
Pears slowly poached in a flavorful broth served along side vanilla ice cream and red wine sauce

Strawberry Cheesecake – 115
Cheesecake topped with fresh strawberry coulis inside a homemade graham cracker crust

Sauce & Garnish

Marinara with a Kick – 121
Simmered fresh tomatoes with fresh and dried herbs and a slightly spicy kick

Tomato Basil Relish – 125
Fresh tomatoes with basil and a light balsamic vinegar dressing

Modern Basil Pesto – 127
A twist on the classic pesto with the addition of cilantro and roasted almonds

For any questions or comments about my food, life, business, or appearances, feel free to send me an email, or visit my website.

JakeTanner@stickitinyourpiehole.com

www.stickitinyourpiehole.com

*New York Sliders w/Parmesan Frico

- Worcestershire - 1 tbs
- Bread crumbs - ⅓ cup
- Eggs - 2
- Olive oil - 2 Tablespoons
- Parmesan cheese - ¼ cup
- Kosher Salt - ½ tsp
- Pepper - 1 tsp
- ~~Parsley~~
- II

Frico
Parmesan cheese - 8 tbs
Pepper - coarse 1 Tbs

Maple & Citrus Marinated Salmon
Glaze - Tuscan Flared

- Salmon - 1½ lbs
- ~~Maple Syrup~~
- lemon - Juice & zest of 1
- Orange ~~Juice~~ - Juice & zest of 1
- Salt - ¼ tsp
- Pepper - ½ tsp

- Maple syrup - ¼ cup
- lemon - Juice & zest of 1
- Orange - Juice & zest of 1
(Slightly Reduced)

Directions 4-14-11
⊠ NO Paper

Roasted chick
- 1 spat

- Rosemary 1 tbs
- Coriander 1 tsp.
- Garlic 10 cloves
- Paprika 1 tsp.
- kSalt 1 tsp
- Pepper 1 tbs
- Olive oil 3 tbs
- Lemon Juice & zest of 1
- Thyme 10 sprigs

Field Green & Pear Salad ⊠Instructions
3-28-11
NO Paper

- Field Greens - 8 cups
- Pear - 1½ Pear
- Candied Pecans - ⅓ cup
- Grapes - ½ cup
- ~~Feta -~~

*Chicken dumplings
- Ground chick
- Soy Sauce
- Sesame oil
- Cilantro
- Scalion
- Pepper ¼

* Grilled Beef Skewers
Instructions ⊠

- Peanut Oil 1 tbs
- Garlic 3 cloves
- Soy Sauce ¼ cup
- Ginger ~~Powder~~ 2 inch piece
- Scallions 1 tbs.
- cilantro 1 tbs.
- Pepper ½ tsp.
- skirt steak 1½ l

Directions ⊠
Chinese ~~style~~ Chop

- 1 ball lettuce Ball
- ¼ cup Almonds
- 2 tbs Cilantro
- ⅓ cup Fried Wonton Pieces
- ⅓ cup Crispy Rice Noodles
- ¼ cup Sesame Seeds

Dressing
1 tsp Sesame oil
1 tsp·1 tbs Soy Sauce

5-25-10 Herb Infuse
- Bread Flour - 3 cup
- Active Dry Yeast - 1
- Sugar - 2 tsp
- Salt - 1 tsp
- Water - 1 cup +
- Olive oil - 2 tbs
- Rosemary - 2 t
- Thyme - 2 t
- Pepper - ½ ts
- Romano ch